I0172330

Great Joy

ADVENT FROM THE GOSPEL OF LUKE

RAY PRITCHARD

Table of Contents

This Advent devotional guide comes from
Keep Believing Ministries.

You can find us on the Internet at
www.KeepBelieving.com.

Questions or Comments?
Email: *ray@keepbelieving.com*

Lord, We Need You!

"I SURVIVED 2024."

Someone could make a fortune selling t-shirts with that slogan. Maybe someone already has. It's been that kind of year:

A contentious national election.
Turmoil in the Middle East.
Economic uncertainty.
The Rise of AI.
Christianity openly mocked.

It has been a hard year.
And it's not over yet.

But before we wrap up 2024 and move on to what we hope are better times, we come to Advent. That's the season that starts around Thanksgiving and leads us to Christmas. Traditionally, it's a time for introspection when we turn the focus away from ourselves and think about our need for Jesus.

Lord, we need you!

We've always needed you.

This year it feels like we need you more than ever.

Our Advent journey starts with the angelic announcement of the birth of Christ:

> *"I bring you good news that will bring great joy to all people"*
> —Luke 2:10 NLT

Good news.
Great joy.
All people.

We could use a full helping of good news and great joy at the end of a challenging year. That's where these Advent devotionals can make a difference. All of them come from the gospel of Luke. I chose Luke because he emphasizes that Christ came for the whole world, including the hurting and the overlooked.

Each devotional ends with a prayer, a QR code, and a link to a YouTube video of a Christmas song. To use the QR code, open your smartphone's camera app and point the camera at the code. Then tap on the link that appears on your screen to go straight to the YouTube video page. I hope you'll take time to read the prayer out loud and then watch the video. Those two things will point your heart in the right direction.

Do you need some good news? Read on. I hope you also find great joy. Remember, Christ came for "all people," which means he came for you.

Let's get started on our journey to Bethlehem.

December 1

The Great Journey Begins

> "In the sixth month, God sent the angel Gabriel to Nazareth, a town in Galilee, to a virgin pledged to be married to a man named Joseph, a descendant of David. The virgin's name was Mary."
>
> — Luke 26-27

IT STARTED WITH AN ANGEL.

That feels exactly right.

The angel comes as a messenger from God to a young girl named Mary. Luke writes the story as if he was a newspaper reporter. To borrow a modern phrase, he reports, we decide. He wants us to know that what happened that day in Nazareth was sober historical reality, not the figment of some writer's imagination.

In the history of the church, Mary has often been portrayed as a kind of misty, otherworldly figure. Some of the great paintings of Mary make her look so peaceful you almost forget she was a real person. That's a shame because Luke makes it clear she had doubts, questions, and deep faith in God. Nowhere is this seen with more clarity than in Luke 1:38:

> "I am the Lord's servant," Mary answered. "May it be to me as you have said."

Without exaggeration, we could call this one of the most remarkable statements in the Bible. We read it so often we forget how great it is. Without warning, she meets Gabriel, who announces she will become pregnant by the Holy Spirit and give birth to the Son of God. When she asks how, he says, "Don't worry about it. The Holy Spirit will cover you like a cloud, and you'll end up pregnant. That's all there is to it."

What do you say to that?

Let's not underestimate what it cost Mary to say Yes to God. From that moment on, she faced the disbelief of her friends ("Oh Mary, how could you expect us to believe such a bizarre story?"), the scurrilous gossip of the neighborhood, and the whispers of promiscuity that have lasted 2,000 years.

Mary knew—or would soon realize—that saying Yes to God meant misunderstanding and public shame. Gone was her pure reputation, and with it her dreams of a quiet, happy life in Nazareth. In the future, her life will be happy many times, but it will never be quiet again.

Mary said yes—yes to God, yes to the impossible, yes to God's will. When the angel said, "*Nothing is impossible with God*" (v. 37), Mary took a deep breath and replied, "*May it be to me as you have said*" (v. 38).

And so the great journey begins.

Grant us faith, O Lord, to believe all you have spoken, even what seems impossible to us. Amen.

Musical Bonus
Let's start our musical journey by listening to a performance of the traditional Advent hymn *O Come, O Come, Emmanuel* by Margaret Becker.
https://youtu.be/MzsDj5kmwoY

December 2

Birthplace of a King

"Joseph also went up from Galilee, from the town of Nazareth, to Judea, to the city of David, which is called Bethlehem, because he was of the house and lineage of David"

— Luke 2:4

IF IT WASN'T THE least likely place, it was very close to it.

Bethlehem was an "on the way" place. You passed through Bethlehem because you were on the way to or from Jerusalem. Bethlehem was indeed a "little town," as described in the familiar Christmas carol by Phillips Brooks. Although well-known as King David's birthplace, the town was home to a few hundred permanent residents. The various inns and guest rooms were full of pilgrims on their way to other places to pay the census tax required by Caesar Augustus (Luke 2:1-3).

When God chose Bethlehem as the birthplace for his Son, he taught us something about the values of heaven. If God had wanted worldly pomp and ceremony, Jesus would have been born in Rome. If he had wanted good standing for his Son, he would have chosen Athens. If he had wanted religious acclaim, he would have chosen Jerusalem.

Or he could have chosen Alexandria or Antioch. The Roman Empire was filled with great cities.

But he chose Bethlehem, an out-of-the-way location. Even in Israel, Bethlehem was "least among the clans of Judah."

But our God is not a frontrunner. He doesn't need worldly power to accomplish his purposes. When Jesus was born, the world paid no attention to a young couple giving birth in a stable in a tiny village in a backwater province of the Roman Empire. No one noticed the baby wrapped in rags sleeping in a feeding trough.

In such an unlikely way, God moved into our neighborhood and became one of us. God's ways are not our ways. If you doubt that, take another look at that sleeping baby. He will one day rule the world.

Joy to the world, the Lord is come!
Let earth receive her King.

O Lord, you are the God of great surprises. Thank you for sending Jesus to save us from our sins. Amen.

Musical Bonus

Musical bonus: Here's an amazing Christmas song filled with God-honoring truth. Check out *Come Behold the Wondrous Mystery* featuring Matt Boswell and Matt Papa. https://youtu.be/h-xQDm-KZw8

Let's Go Straight to Bethlehem!

ADVENT IS A JOURNEY.

We start wherever we are in late November, and by December 25, we end up in Bethlehem.

When the shepherds heard the angels announce that Christ had been born, they said, "*Let's go straight to Bethlehem*" (Luke 2:15 HCSB). I like the way that sounds.

"Let's go." I'm going, and you're going, so let's go together. During the Advent season, Christians of all backgrounds and denominations, from every tribe and tongue, young and old, male and female, rich and poor, all join together to make this journey.

"Straight." No messing around. No detours. No excuses. "We're on our way to see the Savior."

"To Bethlehem." To the "House of Bread," where the Living Bread has come down from heaven. We're coming hungry and thirsty because our journey is long, and we are tired. We're coming to worship the Babe in the manger.

It's good to be in a hurry if you are excited about something that really matters. Nothing in all the world matters more than the birth of Jesus.

That's what Christmas is all about.

When the shepherds heard the news, they went to Bethlehem to check it out for themselves. Luke 2:17 tells us what happened next: "*When they had seen him, they spread the word concerning what had been told them about this child.*" On that night in Bethlehem, outside of Joseph and Mary, the shepherds were the only people who knew Christ had been born.

It wasn't a likely way to win the world. Certainly not the way we would have done it. If we had planned it, Jesus would have been born in Jerusalem to a wealthy family, attended by the high and mighty. That way, no one would doubt the Son of God had come to earth. But God's ways and ours are not the same. He chose to reveal the news to the shepherds first of all. After their initial (and understandable) fear, they responded in faith. They believed the angel and immediately went to Bethlehem, where they found the baby Jesus. Everything was just as the angel said it would be.

I wonder if we would have been as obedient. Would we have believed? Would we have gone to Bethlehem in the middle of the night? Would we have been as quick to tell the story?

Good news is for sharing.

God worked a miracle at Bethlehem.

Don't keep it to yourself.

Lord, keep us watching and waiting for you. Give us the "shepherd spirit" to go quickly to Bethlehem and then tell the world Christ has come. Amen.

Musical Bonus

Musical bonus: I love this version of *Do You Hear What I Hear?* by Mercy Me. You can find it on their album called "It's Christmas!"
https://youtu.be/WWXNOyqTyfQ

Suddenly Angels!

"Suddenly there was with the angel a multitude of the heavenly host praising God"

— Luke 2:13

SUDDENLY!

It means without warning or prior announcement. One moment the angels weren't there, and then they were everywhere. Let me amend that last statement a bit. The word "suddenly" means the angels were nowhere to be seen, and all at once they filled the sky. Some questions come to mind at this point. If we had been there, would we have seen the angels? Could the people in Bethlehem see the angels? Could they be seen in Jerusalem—eight miles away? Could their voices be heard elsewhere, or did the angels reveal themselves only to the shepherds? We cannot fully answer these questions, but this much is certain: The angels were really there, and the shepherds really did hear them.

It is impossible to miss the supernatural element in the birth of Jesus. Angels pop up all over the Christmas story. An angel tells Mary she will give birth to Jesus. An angel tells Joseph to call his name Jesus. An angel warns Mary and Joseph to flee to Egypt. An angel tells them when it's safe to return to Israel. An angel announces the birth of Christ to the shepherds, and then the angelic choir serenades them.

But that's not all. You have the mysterious star that led the Wise Men from some distant land all the way to Bethlehem to the very house where they found the baby Jesus. And the Wise Men were warned in a dream not to return to Herod but to go home another way. So there you have it—angels and stars and dreams. Supernatural stuff everywhere.

We believe something amazing.

Many miracles surround Christmas—the angels, the star, the dreams, the prophecies, and most of all, the virgin birth. Those miracles point to the greatest miracle of all. *We who live in this world have been visited by Someone from the "other world."* Someone from the world of light came to the world of darkness. Someone from the eternal came to the temporary. Someone from heaven came to live with us on earth.

The angels bring good news of great joy, the best news the world has ever heard.

There are more miracles to come on this Advent journey.

Let's pray for faith to believe all over again as we get ready for Christmas this year.

*Lord Jesus, open our hearts so that we will believe
everything you have said. Amen.*

Musical Bonus
Recently I heard a Christmas carol that was new to me (although it was first published in 1684). I love this version because the video includes the lyrics. I hope you enjoy this arrangement of the Sussex Carol.
https://youtu.be/-0XfVqSiPDo

Good News for Sinners

"It is not the healthy who need a doctor, but the sick"
— Luke 5:31

ARE YOU SICK?

If so, you might need a doctor.

The pandemic reminded us how fragile we are and how thin the line is between sickness and health. You can feel great today and come down with a virus tomorrow.

That's when you need a doctor.

The next verse clarifies what Jesus meant: "*I did not come to call the righteous, but sinners to repentance*" (v. 32). If you think you are righteous, you will not see your need for a Savior. But if you know you are a sinner, you will run to the cross.

That's why some people have trouble with Jesus. They don't take that "I'm a sinner" business seriously. I remember reading about an evangelist who worked in New Orleans. God gave him a powerful ministry to the musicians, singers, barkers, gamblers and prostitutes who frequented the famous French Quarter. He said he had always found it easy to win prostitutes to Christ because they already knew they were sinners. You don't have to convince them of that. All you have to do is show them love and give them hope for a better life.

He said it was much harder to win Baptist deacons because they have so much religion they don't think they need to be saved. Are prostitutes worse sinners than Baptist deacons? No, not really. *They both need Jesus.* But one thinks he's good enough; the other knows she's not. That's why it's easier to win a prostitute than a deacon to Christ.

Religious people are offended by the simplicity of salvation. *When sinners hear the gospel, they know it is their only chance to go to heaven.*

How do we receive God's gift of salvation? Simply by asking for it. Do you want Christ in your life? You may have him today! This is the wonder of the gospel. Do not say, "I'll do my best and come to Christ later." That is the language of hell. You cannot be saved as long as you hold on to your notions of goodness.

If you are sick with sin, Jesus is the Great Physician you need. That's the promise God made when he sent his Son to be our Savior.

Lord Jesus, thank you for grace that saves sinners
because that's my only hope of heaven. Amen.

Musical Bonus

Today's video features a group called Sixpence None the Richer. They produced a version of *Silent Night* that is bound to lift your spirits. https://youtu.be/N6ml_YbgJsQ

Turning Tears into Laughter

"Blessed are you who weep now, because you will laugh"
— Luke 6:21

WE MIGHT CALL THIS the blessing no one wants.

It is a paradox and a mystery.

Jesus promises that those who weep now will laugh later. That sounds good, but when do we get to the laughter part?

We have a long list of friends who live in the first part of this verse. One friend struggles because her cancer has come back. Another friend has children who have become prodigals. Another friend tries to find her way after her husband unexpectedly died a year ago.

Such is life in a fallen world.

Suffering turns us to the Lord as nothing else can. Perhaps you've heard it said this way, "You never know if Jesus is all you need until Jesus is all you have. But when Jesus is all you have, then and only then will you discover that Jesus really is all you need." Recently we received a letter from a prisoner named Monica, who said,

> I finished reading *An Anchor for the Soul,* and I am about to begin reading it again. I truly believe I have been blessed by the situation I am currently in. Because of it, I know I have gained eternal life with Jesus. If I had not been arrested, I doubt I would have ever come to know Jesus as I do now.

Prison is not "good" in the usual sense of the word, but going to jail can be good if it causes us to turn to the Lord. So it is with all life's troubles, difficulties, and afflictions. *We pray more, and we pray more fervently during a time of crisis because we know if God doesn't help us, we're sunk.* God allows hard things to happen to his children to get our attention focused entirely on him.

Even in the most difficult moments, God's people can rejoice because he is at work doing something important in them. More than one person has told me, "I wouldn't trade my pain for the things God has shown me." If that doesn't make sense, it is only because you haven't been there yet.

God is good, and his mercy endures forever. He proved it by sending his Son. Christmas is God's guarantee the darkness won't last forever and that someday God will wipe all our tears away. Meanwhile, we press on, waiting for the happy laughter of heaven.

Chin up, child of God. The best is yet to come!

My God, thank you for hope that death cannot destroy. Thank you for Jesus because his coming changed everything. Amen.

Musical Bonus
While researching this project, I stumbled upon the most stunning Christmas song I've ever heard. It carries the unlikely title of *O Come, All You Unfaithful*, but it is filled with the Good News of Jesus.
https://youtu.be/C-QHbpYjuIg

His Kingdom Will Never End

"His kingdom will never end"

— Luke 1:33

IT IS EASY TO FORGET how revolutionary these words must have sounded in the beginning.

They were …

Spoken by an angel
To a virgin
Announcing a baby
Who will one day
Rule the world.

It happened in Nazareth, a tiny village in Galilee. On that day, you would have said the mighty Roman Empire would last forever. But it had been preceded by many other empires:

Egypt
Assyria
Babylon
Medo-Persia
Greece

A visit to imperial Rome might convince you it would last a thousand years. But a few centuries later, the empire disintegrated.

So the angel's words didn't seem likely.

How would Mary's baby have a kingdom that never ends?

They were just a young couple facing a crisis pregnancy. The whole affair would cast a shadow over them and lead to rumors and insinuations that would follow Jesus during his earthly ministry.

Even now, after 2000 years, the angel's message seems mind-blowing. What a series of predictions he made. As I thought about those improbable words, I found myself singing these words from the Hallelujah Chorus:

The kingdom of this world
Is become the kingdom of our Lord,
And of his Christ, and of his Christ;
And he shall reign forever and ever,
Forever and ever, forever and ever.

Jesus is building his kingdom in human hearts around the world. Someday he will return and visibly reign on the earth. That kingdom—his kingdom—will never end.

The followers of Jesus are the ultimate revolutionaries because they have concluded only one thing will never end . . .**His kingdom**

Some men and women are not like everyone else. They believe the kingdom of God is the greatest thing in the world and that one thought has revolutionized everything they do. Kingdom issues are at stake. That's the only possible explanation for the way they live.

Everyone reading these words has a choice to make. Join the kingdoms of this world that are doomed to fail. Or join forces with Jesus Christ and follow him as your Savior and Lord.

His kingdom will never end. Why would you follow anyone else?

Lord Jesus, your kingdom is the only one that will last forever.
Help me to live by kingdom values today. Amen.

Musical Bonus
What do you get when you mix Handel's
Messiah with contemporary Christian music?
You get *For Unto Us/Open the Eyes of My Heart*
by Paul Baloche.
https://youtu.be/9ue6FbiHf30

December 8

The Biggest Family on Earth

"My mother and my brothers are those who hear and do the word of God"

— Luke 8:21

WHERE IS HOME FOR YOU?

If you live long enough and move around enough, the answer to that question will be a moving target. When I was growing up, my home was a small town in Alabama. Marlene and I have moved ten times in fifty years. That seems like a lot until you realize the Census Bureau says the average American moves 11.7 times.

On a trip to Atlanta, I called Marlene and left a message saying I was looking forward to coming home. I didn't mean I was looking forward to the house where we were living. When I got home, I didn't hug the drapes and say, "Drapes, I'm glad to see you." I didn't say to the rug, "Oh, rug, I missed you so much." The house is beautiful, but it is home because the people I love live there. Home to me is where they are, and if they are not there, it doesn't seem like home at all.

That truth underlies the words of Jesus in Luke 8:21.

God's family is huge, and it includes everyone who believes in Jesus. It's not limited to one race or one culture or one nationality. That's the mistake some Jews made in the first century. They thought being a physical descendant of Abraham made them part of God's family. But God doesn't judge by the name on the birth certificate. He checks your spiritual DNA. Do you know Jesus? Have you trusted him as your Savior? Do you follow his teaching?

Christ came to bring you into God's Forever Family. You can be at home anywhere on earth because God has his people everywhere.

I was part of a group that visited a house church in China. There were perhaps 50 people crowded into a tiny apartment. We began by singing and praying for 40 minutes. Then I preached. Then we sang some more, followed by exhortations from the pastor. It was a long service by American standards, but the people were in no hurry to go home. When we finished, everyone stayed for lunch, laughing, talking, and sharing. Although I know very little Chinese, I felt right at home. They welcomed us as if we had known them forever. That's the way it's supposed to be.

When you follow Jesus, you meet his brothers and sisters wherever you go. Then when you die, you meet him face to face. What a deal! Nothing on earth could top that.

Spirit of God, thank you for making me part of a family so large that it will take eternity to meet all my brothers and sisters. Amen.

Musical Bonus
Suppose you took the melody of "Come Thou Fount" and gave it Christmas lyrics. Would that work? A group called We Are Messengers took that challenge and produced a gospel-centered Christmas song called *This is Jesus*. https://youtu.be/hAsmsVudnrU

Unlimited Supply

"They picked up twelve baskets of leftover pieces"
— Luke 9:17

THE DISCIPLES HAD A BIG PROBLEM.

The disciples had a big problem.

How do you feed 5000 hungry men? That would require an army of food trucks and an enormous army of cooks and servers. To make matters worse, the disciples had five loaves of bread and two fish. That wouldn't feed five people, much less 5000.

So Jesus worked a miracle.

First, the disciples organized the crowd. This made it easier to serve the people. It meant that in Jesus' mind, the miracle had already been done. After giving thanks, he broke the bread. This is where the miracle took place—in his hands. As the disciples watched him break the bread, it miraculously multiplied until all were fed. The disciples served as waiters. This ensured their faith would grow as they participated in the miracle Jesus was performing.

The disciples also had a few small fish. Jesus blessed the fish, multiplied them, and had the disciples serve the people.

No one went away hungry.

Everyone had all they wanted.

There were plenty of leftovers.

This was not an airline meal, and it wasn't a snack or a box lunch. *Omnipotence has an unending supply.* When Jesus serves the meal, there is always enough to go around with plenty left over. What a lesson for the disciples to learn.

Never fear to trust him.

What do you need today?

He has more than enough mercy, more than enough grace, and more than enough power.

Jesus came to earth as the Living Bread from heaven. Fear not. He has enough to meet your need, with plenty for tomorrow.

Lord Jesus, when my cupboard is bare, remind me that your pantry is always full. Teach me to trust when I can't see how I will make it through another day. Amen.

Musical Bonus
Let's listen as Faith Hill sings a beautiful arrangement of *O Come, All Ye Faithful.*
https://youtu.be/Ok6IBzG8m-A

December 10

My Good Samaritan

"He went over to him and bandaged his wounds, pouring on olive oil and wine"

— Luke 10:34

WE DON'T KNOW HIS NAME.

We call him the "Good Samaritan" because that's what he was. Unlike the priest and the Levite who walked by on the other side, this hated Samaritan cared enough to get involved. He had as many reasons to pass by on the other side, but he didn't.

He saw the man.

He bandaged his wounds.

He poured on oil and wine.

Then he took him to an inn where the man could get the help he needed. He even gave the innkeeper money and promised to return later and pay for any extra expenses.

Here is the kicker: The two men who should have shown compassion didn't, and the one who wouldn't have been expected to did. The religious leaders knew the truth and did nothing about it. The Samaritan was an outcast, but he knew the truth, and his compassion moved him to action.

Once upon a time, a man fell into a pit and couldn't get himself out. A sensitive person came along and said, "I feel for you down there." A practical person came along and said, "I knew you were going to fall in sooner or later." A Pharisee said, "Only bad people fall into a pit." A mathematician calculated how far he fell. A news reporter wanted an exclusive story on his pit. An IRS agent asked if he was paying taxes on the pit. A self-pitying person said, "You haven't seen anything until you've seen my pit." A mystic said, "Just imagine you're not in a pit." An optimist said, "Things could be worse." A pessimist said, "Things will get worse." When Jesus saw the man, he took him by the hand and lifted him out of the pit.

Jesus is our Good Samaritan. He had mercy on us when we were left for dead by the side of the road. Here is a message for those who are still lying by the road, wounded and bleeding, forgotten and abandoned. This story is for those who have been destroyed by sin. Jesus comes to help you. Will you not give him your heart? Will you not love him and trust him and serve him? Will you not believe in him? The Good Samaritan comes to save you. Will you not trust him as Lord and Savior?

He has already come for you.

He is waiting for you to come to him.

Lord Jesus, thank you for being my Good Samaritan. When everyone else passed by on the other side, you came from heaven to rescue me. Amen.

Musical Bonus
Brandon Heath has recorded a new Christmas song called *King of Kings.*
https://youtu.be/CQG3wrQ3EfE

Shameless Prayer

"Because of his friend's shameless boldness, he will get up and give him as much as he needs"
— Luke 11:8

WHAT KIND OF FRIEND knocks on your door at midnight?

If I hear a knock in the middle of the night, especially in these troubled times, I'm going to think twice about going to the door. A robber wouldn't typically knock at all. He would find an open window or an unlocked door, or he would break the glass and then come in.

Robbers don't usually announce themselves.

This story reminds me of the old saying, "Nothing good happens after midnight." That strikes me as a reliable bit of wisdom. Since this was written 2000 years ago, Luke doesn't mention phone calls or text messages. As I think about it, I don't believe I've ever gotten a phone call at 2 AM where someone said, "Pastor Ray, I've got some good news." It's always bad news when they call that late.

The knock on the door is even worse.

But what if, after taking due precautions, when you go to the door, you discover it's not a burglar or a troublemaker, and it's not the police with bad news?

It's your friend, and he needs some bread. One of *his* friends needs three loaves of bread, and your friend has none. He is asking for bread for his friend at midnight.

In Jesus' story, the man tells his friend, "Don't bother me!" But the friend won't be put off. He keeps on knocking because he is "shameless" in his request. Though it strains your friendship, Jesus said the man will get up and give his friend whatever he needs.

So it is when we pray.

Jesus is <u>not</u> saying God gets irritated with us. He means if shameless requests can turn hard hearts on earth, how much more will our persistent prayer move the heart of God who already loves us.

Don't be ashamed to pray. *Ask God for whatever you need.* Remember, he knows your heart before you open your mouth. If you need three loaves of bread, ask for them. If you need a miracle, ask for one. There's no extra charge for large requests.

The door to heaven is wide open. Knock, knock, and keep on knocking. Soon the door will be opened to you.

*Lord Jesus, give me grace to keep on praying when
it would be easy to give up. Amen.*

Musical Bonus
Paul Cardall and Audrey Assad recorded a gorgeous arrangement of
In the Bleak Midwinter.
https://youtu.be/Zw4542p2tMo

24

More Than Sparrows

"You are worth more than many sparrows"
— Luke 12:7

WHO THINKS ABOUT SPARROWS?

If you check your Bible dictionary, you'll discover that sparrows were among the humblest birds in Bible times. They were considered food for the poor, and because they were so cheap, the poor could offer them in sacrifice to the Lord if they couldn't afford a lamb or a goat or a bull. You could buy two sparrows for a penny. That's cheap by any standard. A buck would buy you a whole bag full of sparrows. You could feed your family sparrow casserole for a dime. (A friend from India told me he used to hunt sparrows and eat them. "They were better than chicken," he said. I'll take his word for it.)

Think of it this way.

God sees the sparrows.

He numbers the sparrows.

He notices the sparrows.

When the sparrow falls to the ground, it happens because God willed it to fall, and if he didn't, the sparrow would never fall to the ground. This is a high view of God's involvement in the tiny details of the universe. Even the falling of the sparrow is part of God's providential oversight of the universe. This applies to our personal pain and to the heartache of watching our loved ones suffer.

I got a message from some friends who are going through a severe medical crisis. They have been battling cancer for a long time, and no one knows what the future may hold. The husband wrote to say he struggles to understand how everything works together for good in this circumstance. I told him we see only bits and pieces of God's plan. Sometimes those bits and pieces don't make much sense to us. I am comforted by these words of Alva J. McClain: "From the fall of a raindrop to the fall of an empire, all is under the providential control of God." If we believe that, we can keep going even though fears and doubts assail us.

Since we are worth more than "many sparrows" to God, if he cares for them, will he not care for us, too? Why should we shake? Why should we fear? Let the world shake and fear.

As the song says, "His eye is on the sparrow, and I know he watches me."

Thank you, Gracious Lord, for watching over the tiny sparrows. When I am afraid, I will trust in you. Amen.

Musical Bonus

If you need encouragement in these troubled times, check out *Make Room* by Casting Crowns.
https://youtu.be/iUFSxt7qkNw

December 13

When God Throws a Party

"People will come from east and west and north and south, and will take their places at the feast in the kingdom of God"

— Luke 13:29

WHEN GOD THROWS A PARTY, he invites people from everywhere.

Jesus said they will come streaming in from north, south, east and west. Think about what this means:

God intends to have Bolivians in heaven.
He wants Koreans at his banquet table.
He calls them from the islands of the Pacific.
He intends to save people from Kosovo.
He wants Russians at his table.
He wants Chinese at his banquet.
He calls them from Canada and Sweden.
He invites them from Nepal and Tibet.
He intends to have Moroccans feasting with him.
He wants Turks there.
He calls Iraqis and Israelis.
He wants a host of believers from Irian Jaya at his table.

Heaven will be filled with people of every language, culture, skin color, and ethnic background gathered to praise the Lord who saved them.

As someone has said, there will be three surprises when we get to heaven:

<u>First</u>, we will be surprised to find some people we never expected to see in heaven.

<u>Second</u>, we will be surprised some people we expected to see in heaven are not there.

<u>Third</u>, the greatest surprise will be that we are there.

When we see the glories of heaven with all the saints and angels gathered there, the greatest surprise will be that we can take part in that grand celebration.

Christmas is the end of thinking we can save ourselves. The birth of Christ means God has come to earth on the greatest rescue mission in history.

The sequence of events that unfolded—the census, the long journey, no room at the inn, "no crib for a bed," the feeding trough, the "swaddling clothes"—all of it was planned by God even though it all appeared to happen by chance. God willed there would be no room in the inn not for the sake of Jesus but for our sake so that we might learn who Jesus is and why he came.

God always intended to include men and women from the north, south, east, and west. Be glad God included you!

"For God so loved the world" is still true today.

Lord Jesus, thank you for making me part of your worldwide family.
Amen.

Musical Bonus

If you like bluegrass music, you'll enjoy this down-home version of *God Rest Ye Merry, Gentlemen.*
https://music.youtube.com/watch?v=sEdthrnMGUo

December 14

Room for One More

"Go out to the roads and country lanes and compel them to come in, so that my house may be full"
— Luke 14:23

THERE IS GOOD NEWS and bad news in this story.

Let's start with the bad news. Some people don't want to come to the big party. They were on the list, they received an invitation, but they turned it down. One fellow had a field that needed tending, so he begged off. That's understandable. If you have a field, you've got to watch it constantly. Farming is a nonstop business. So it makes sense that tending a field would come first.

There was a second man, also a farmer, who had just purchased five oxen. That was no small investment in the first century. Someone had to see if they could stay in the harness and pull the plow.

Finally, there was a third man who had just gotten married. Probably he and his bride had already been through a round of parties, and they wanted some time alone. Who could blame them?

What's the problem? These are all legitimate excuses, aren't they? Yes, but no excuse matters when the Lord does the inviting.

No wonder the host was indignant. I would be angry if my guests stiffed me like that.

But there is good news here. The host ordered his servants to find the lame, the crippled, and the infirm. And there was still room at the master's table.

Every seat must be filled!

The host sent his servants into the highways and byways to find anyone who would come to the great feast. This story cuts both ways. Those who refuse to come will be left out, but anyone who wants to be there can find a seat.

Here is good news for the world. Christ didn't die for good people because there aren't any. He died for sinners and rebels and scoundrels. If you qualify in any of those categories, you can be saved.

Christmas means there is hope for all of us. If the scribes don't want to come to Bethlehem, make room for the shepherds. If Herod hates Jesus, the Wise Men worship him.

"Where meek souls will receive him still,
The dear Christ enters in."

There is always room for one more.

Spirit of God, we pray for those who feel forgotten this Christmas season. Help them to know they are always welcome at the Father's table. Amen.

Musical Bonus
Valaura Arnold asks us to think about the hurting people all around us in this moving version of *Sweet Little Jesus Boy.*
https://music.youtube.com/
watch?v=MNNLJ3B_y1Y

December 15

Hope for the Prodigal

"For this son of mine was dead and is alive again; he was lost and is found"

— Luke 15:24

IT IS POSSIBLE TO KNOW *God and yet be far from him.*

Most Christians know what that is like. Perhaps you have had the experience of drifting away from God. You never meant it to happen, but somewhere along the way, you made some wrong choices, and one day, you woke up to find that you were far away from God.

This happens irrespective of your spiritual pedigree. You might be an elder or a deacon and still be far from God. You might be a Sunday School teacher, a youth leader, an usher, a member of the choir, a Bible Institute student, and still be far from God. You may have been raised in a Christian home only to grow up and reject your heritage. You may have been deeply hurt by someone who claimed to be a Christian, and that deep hurt has kept you from coming close to God. You may have decided no one can truly live up to what the Bible commands. Perhaps you feel discouraged over repeated personal failure. You tried and tried and tried, and finally, exhausted, you gave up.

Something like that happened to the prodigal son.

He left his family and wasted his inheritance in the "far country." Only then, having lost everything that mattered to him, did he wake up and begin the long journey home. He must have wondered how he would be received.

It's certainly easy to criticize the prodigal son. But I will tell you at least one good thing about this young man. *When the time came to*

31

move, he moved. He didn't let the grass grow under his feet. So many people say, "Tomorrow I will arise and go to my father. Next year, next day, next month. Give me some time to think about it." This man said, "I am going to go." And he got up and went right then.

He needn't have worried about his reception because his father ran to greet him. It is a parable of Christmas. We are all prodigals running from the grace of God. Left to ourselves, we will die in our sins. But God would not leave us alone.

Jesus left heaven to save a race of prodigal sons and daughters. Do you know someone in the "far country" of sin? Keep praying and keep believing.

Light shines from Bethlehem to point the way on the long journey home.

Almighty God, we pray today for those who are far from you. Give us faith to keep praying until our prodigals finally come home. Amen.

Musical Bonus
We have a special treat today. If you need some inspiration, I hope you'll listen as Sara Evans performs *Go Tell It on the Mountain*.
https://youtu.be/vcyHXc7Wv48

December 16

Jesus' Investment Advice

"Use worldly wealth to gain friends for yourself, so that when it is gone, you will be welcomed into eternal dwellings"

— Luke 16:9

LET'S CALL THIS JESUS' INVESTMENT ADVICE.

We should use our worldly wealth to make friends for ourselves. That's what the unjust steward did.

Notice the reason he gives—"So that when it is gone." What is the "it" Jesus is talking about? Money and everything money can buy. Money fails. Five minutes after you are dead, somebody else will have your money. Five minutes after death, your checkbook will be useless to you. On that day, it won't matter whether you lived in a mansion with a swimming pool or in a hovel on the wrong side of the tracks.

Think of it. All you live for, the accumulated wealth of a lifetime, everything you dreamed about, every cent you ever saved, every investment, all of it gone forever. It fails you in the end.

After a rich man dies, people often say, "How much did he leave?" The answer is always the same.

He left all of it.

The question is not, "How much did you make?" The question is, "How did you spend what you had while you had it?" Did you buy houses, land, stocks, furniture, new cars, new clothes? Was that the goal of your life? Or did you make friends for God with your money?

Those are your only two choices.

The issue is not getting rich versus staying poor. *It's not between the stock market and Jesus.* The issue is this: How did you use the money you made? Did you get rich for your own sake, or did you use your wealth to make friends for God?

Jesus said you should use your money to gain friends who will welcome you into "eternal dwellings." That's heaven. Jesus is saying we should use our money to make sure people get to heaven so that they will welcome us when we get there.

Will anyone be glad to see you in heaven? Will anyone hug your neck and say, "Thanks for making sure I got here?" Will anyone be there because you made friends for God with your money? When you pass through the pearly gates, will there be a standing ovation from the people you helped in this life? Or will all the things you spent your money on be left behind?

When Christ was born, God turned the values of the world upside down. Let's invest in Christ's kingdom because it's the only thing that will last forever.

O Lord, save us from investing in things that will not last. Help us to live so that in 10,000 years we will have no regrets. Amen.

Musical Bonus
Phillips, Craig and Dean give a country twist to their version of
How Great Our Joy/ Joy to the World.
https://www.youtube.com/
watch?v=fQBWehFm3lY

December 17

Mulberry Faith

"You can say to this mulberry tree, 'Be uprooted and planted in the sea"
— Luke 17:6

AGGRESSIVE.

That's the word they use for the roots of the mulberry tree. The roots are so aggressive they can uproot a sidewalk. That's why Jesus used this figure of speech. Some plants can be easily pulled out of the ground.

Not a mulberry tree.

Once you plant it, you won't be able to move it easily.

But there is a way it can be moved. You need faith the size of a mustard seed, the smallest common seed in the Holy Land. It is only 1-2 millimeters in diameter, meaning it's about as thick as a credit card.

A tiny bit of faith can uproot a mulberry tree and plant it in the sea. That's the lesson Jesus gave to his disciples when they said, "**Lord, increase our faith**" (Luke 17:5). In one sense, this is hyperbole. *Jesus uses an absurdity to point out the great possibilities of prayer.* It's not as if Jesus is saying, "Peter, you can do this. You can take this mulberry tree and plant it in the Mediterranean Sea." That's not the meaning. Peter couldn't do it, neither could James or John or any of the apostles. It was a total impossibility. *But it wasn't impossible for God!* That's the whole point.

What's the hardest part about casting a mulberry tree into the sea? Most people would probably answer, *"Having faith"* or *"Not doubting in your heart."* The hardest part is having the courage to talk to the mulberry tree in the first place. What kind of person looks at a tree and talks to it? If you do that on a regular basis, people will begin to question your sanity. Yet that's precisely what Jesus tells his disciples they must do.

No prayer offered in faith can ever fail. Sometimes God answers exactly as we have prayed. Often his answers come in a different fashion. The answer may be delayed, or the Lord may substitute something better, or he may give us grace to bear what we asked might be removed from our lives. Yet in all this, God still answers prayer.

God always answers believing prayer. Always!

Are we willing to believe what Jesus said? *You can never command a mulberry tree to be planted in the sea by yourself, but God can.* So ask him! Ask him to do what only he can do.

Remember what the angel said to Mary, "**Nothing is impossible with God**" (Luke 1:37). *So let the people of God keep on praying.* Claim God's promises. Say to the mulberry tree, "Be cast into the sea." Then stand back and see what the Lord will do.

Heavenly Father, give me mulberry faith when I feel like giving up because nothing is impossible with you. Amen.

Musical Bonus
Here's a French carol that dates to the 1830s.
Let's listen as Josh Groban (with Brian McKnight) sings
Angels We Have Heard on High.
https://youtu.be/dtByTy_5jqI

December 18

Praying in the Last Days

"When the Son of Man comes, will he find faith on the earth?"

— Luke 18:8

WHAT A QUESTION!

In Luke 18:1-7 Jesus tells the story of the widow who persisted and got her way when mistreated by an unjust judge. He kept ignoring her, but her persistence wore him down. The moral of the story is obvious. Keep praying.

Then he asked a surprising question:

Will Jesus find faith on the earth when he returns?

There will be a massive turning away from the Lord in the last days. It is sometimes called the "apostasy" or the "falling away." You can read about it in Matthew 24, Mark 13, Luke 21, and 2 Thessalonians 2. As we rush headlong toward the return of Christ, we should expect to see precisely what is happening today:

False Christs.

Spiritual counterfeits.

Christians compromising their faith.

Pastors turning away from the truth.

As the foundations of society crumble beneath us, we will see this happening more and more. All these things are the **"beginning of sorrows"** (Matthew 24:8 KJV). In a world where truth has become entirely subjective, where feelings trump biblical commands, where we reinterpret the Bible to justify our sin, Jesus' poignant question takes on a deeper meaning:

> When the Son of Man comes…
> Will he find faith in your church?
> Will he find faith in your family?
> Will he find faith in your heart?

As we journey through life, there will always be some prayers that haven't been answered yet. Will we give up, or will we keep praying? That's what Jesus means when he asks, **"When the Son of Man comes, will he find faith on the earth?"**

Will he find anyone still believing, or will everyone turn away?

Will he find faithful believers who still pray as the world self-destructs?

Jesus is coming soon. All the signs point to the same conclusion: "It won't be long now."

Jesus came the first time as a baby in Bethlehem.

He will come the second time as the conquering King.

God help us to pray in faith while we wait for Jesus to come again.

Almighty God, grant that we might not be discouraged even a little bit by the things that happen around us. Grant us grace to keep on praying and not to faint. Amen.

Musical bonus

Some people call *Away in a Manger* "Luther's Cradle Hymn," but the original author has been lost to history. In 2016, Sarah McLachlan produced this soft jazz version of Away in a Manger. Enjoy!
https://youtu.be/zleH5tesZaQ

December 19

The Stones Will Cry Out

"Some of the Pharisees in the crowd said to Jesus, 'Teacher, rebuke your disciples!'"

— Luke 19:39

SOME PEOPLE CAN'T BE HAPPY if someone else is happy.

The Pharisees didn't like people cheering as Jesus rode into Jerusalem. It was too raucous, too spontaneous, and way over the top. Even the children were cheering for Jesus.

And what's up with those palm fronds?

No doubt the final straw was hearing the people cry out, "Blessed is he who comes in the name of the Lord." That bordered on blasphemy, or so they thought. That's why the Pharisees wanted Jesus to rebuke his disciples.

But he didn't.

The cheering crowds warmed his heart because it meant they understood why he had entered Jerusalem riding on a donkey. If they didn't know everything about him, they knew he was more than a regular rabbi. He entered Jerusalem like a king!

Jesus' response teaches us something important: **"If they keep quiet, the stones will cry out"** (v. 40). This is God's world, and he will be praised by the world he has made. If men and women will not do it, the rocks themselves will sing praise to the Lord.

We all understand that public displays of faith are frowned upon by the powers that be. They are fine if we praise the Lord behind closed doors, but don't you dare take it to the streets. Keep your songs to yourself, hold down the noise, and don't disturb the peace.

If you do make a ruckus, you might find yourself in court. Or perhaps in jail.

There is nothing new under the sun. When Jesus was born, Herod tried to kill him, and if not for a midnight flight to Egypt, he might have succeeded. People hated Jesus then, and they hate him now.

But Jesus paid no attention to the Pharisees.

He welcomed the praise of the children.

Our God deserves praise. Loud praise! Public praise! Exuberant praise! If we will not do our part, the rocks will cry out in praise to the Lord.

If some people don't like your praise, don't let them bully you into silence.

Open your mouth and sing to the Lord!

As he enters and exits the world, Jesus is both attacked and praised. Let's make sure we stand with those who praise him openly.

If you believe Jesus is the Savior of the world, come with an open heart, bow down before the Lord Jesus, and worship him. As the hymn says, "Come and worship. Come and worship. Worship Christ the newborn King."

Spirit of God, give us the simple faith of a child that we, too, might openly sing the praises of Jesus. Amen.

Musical Bonus

Planetshakers produced a beautiful version of a familiar carol. Let's listen to *O Holy Night.* https://youtu.be/A_Yn7rEAHfo

December 20

Why Christ Came

WHY DID CHRIST come to the earth?

It is not enough to know who Jesus is. *By and large, the world knows what Christians believe about Jesus.* But what the world wants to know is this: Why did he come, and what difference does it make?

Many answers have been given to that question. Some argue Jesus came to give us an example of God's love. Others say he was the Perfect Man, the shining example that can lift the rest of us up. Many people consider him the greatest teacher of all time. Still others believe he came to establish a new religion. Some scholars say he was a reformist rabbi who wanted to start a movement to purify Israel.

Against all the theories of men, we have the clear words of our Lord himself:

"For the Son of Man came to seek and to save what was lost"
(Luke 19:10).

The word "lost" has almost gone out of style in Christian circles. We talk of being estranged from God, of being confused about our purpose in life, about needing a new beginning. All of that is true, but it is hard to improve on the simple Bible word "lost."

Search the pages of God's book from cover to cover. Read everything from Adam's sin in Genesis to the final battle in Revelation. Then pick up the morning newspaper and see if you don't agree with Jesus.

Men and women are lost without God.

You will never understand who Jesus is until you realize he came to save you from your sins. This is why he lived, this is why he died, and this is why he rose from the dead. He came to seek and to save the lost. And he saves all those who trust in him.

If our greatest need had been education, God would have sent a teacher.

If our greatest need had been money, God would have sent a banker.

If our greatest need had been advice, God would have sent a counselor.

But since our greatest need was forgiveness, God sent a Savior. His name is Jesus. He is Christ the Lord, the Son of God who came from heaven to earth.

God has more grace in his heart than you have sin in your life.

Jesus is a better Savior than you are a sinner.

When you come to Jesus, you will find that he has already come for you.

Mighty Savior, you came to seek and to save the lost. We gladly say, "Welcome to our world." We need you more than we know. Amen.

Musical Bonus

Terrian Bass Woods is a vocalist in TobyMac's band DiverseCity. Here is the official music video of her hit single *God With Us.*
https://youtu.be/PJbtWOSYjBM

December 21

Peace in Perilous Times

"When you hear about wars and riots, don't be afraid"
— Luke 21:9

WE LIVE IN STRANGE TIMES

Someone has called this the Age of Anxiety, and it seems fitting. Not long ago I found this headline: "Most Think Country Headed in Wrong Direction." Those words could be slightly altered to read like this:

"Most Think Family Headed in Wrong Direction."
"Most Think Marriage Headed in Wrong Direction."
"Most Think World Headed in Wrong Direction

Such is life right now.

Jesus Christ had a word for times like these. On the Wednesday before he was crucified, he met with his disciples to prepare them for what was to come. Under the shadow of the temple, he told them what the world would be like after he was gone. In that message, he included these famous words: **"When you hear about wars and riots, don't be afraid"** (Luke 21:9 CEV). The Living Bible offers this paraphrase: "When you hear of wars and insurrections beginning, don't panic." Those are the words of a madman, or they are the words of the Son of God.

If we panic, it means we have forgotten who runs the universe.

Jesus even said, **"These things must happen"** (v. 9). The unrest in our cities didn't catch him by surprise. He knew about the election controversy before it happened. The Lord is seated on his throne. He's not pacing the floor, worried about the future.

Hard times are upon us. They are part of the course of this age: wars and rumors of wars, natural disasters, strange viruses. They will only get worse in the days ahead.

But we have Jesus' words—"Don't panic." But who wouldn't panic? Only those who know that God is in control. *When the world seems to be self-destructing, our faith shows itself to be real.*

Christmas means God has not left us alone in the world. He came to visit us one dark night 2,000 years ago.

The glory of God shines forth from the manger in Bethlehem.

His glory still shines today.

One day his glory will fill the earth.

For those who believe in Jesus, the best is yet to come.

Christians ought to be the calmest people on earth because we know the Lord, and he holds the future in his hands. There is no panic in heaven. You will lose your perspective if you spend all your time perusing the latest news. Focus on the Lord, remember his promises, and all will be well.

Sovereign Lord, you are the firm foundation beneath our feet. We trust in you, and we will not be moved. When the kingdoms of the earth crumble to dust, your words will still be true. Amen.

Musical Bonus
The group Rend Collective (along with Keith and Kristyn Getty) produced a new version of an older carol with a bit of whimsy added: *We Three Kings (We're Not Lost)*.
https://youtu.be/Tp83tnTSl0Y

December 22

Strange Way to Be Born

> "How will this be" Mary asked the angel, "since I am a virgin?"
>
> — Luke 1:34

CHRISTMAS IS ALMOST HERE.

That's a relief.

So much has happened that we wouldn't be surprised to read this headline: "Christmas Canceled Because of Middle East Conflict." It's been that kind of year.

But Christmas has not been canceled.

We're only three days away from the celebration of Jesus' birth. Some things can't be changed by the rush of current events. No one in Judea expected the birth of the Messiah 2000 years ago. If Twitter had existed back then, they would have been debating the legality of the census ordered by Caesar Augustus. That's the one that forced people to travel back to their hometowns. No doubt people would have argued against it and tried to organize a boycott.

Good luck with that.

The Romans took a dim view of boycotts and public demonstrations.

But the greater point remains. No one knew or expected or even imagined what was about to happen. There were no Christmas trees in Bethlehem.

What happened there remains the central mystery of the Christian faith. The angel told Joseph to call the baby Immanuel because that's who Jesus is—God with us. He stripped off his royal robes and exchanged them for strips of peasant cloth. He traded a palace for a stable so that he might be "God with us."

Here's how one Statement of Faith puts it: "We believe in the deity of Jesus Christ, that He was conceived of the Holy Spirit, born of the Virgin Mary, lived a sinless life, and is fully God and fully Man." That sentence contains a phrase that will make the smartest man stop and scratch his head: "fully God and fully man." *How that could be is a mystery to us.* By that phrase, we mean that the baby in the manger was God in human flesh.

See his little hands and feet; they are the hands and feet of God.

Listen to him laugh; it is the laughter of God.

Wipe the tears from his infant cheeks; you are wiping the tears of God.

Some things we understand and therefore believe. *Christmas is a miracle of another order.* We can think of a thousand other ways God could have done it. But God chose the unusual (a virgin birth) and the unlikely (a baby born in a stable) as his means of visiting our planet.

At Christmastime, like the Wise Men of old, we are invited to bring our gifts to Bethlehem and welcome God to our world.

Father, we believe in the virgin birth because we believe your Word. As we contemplate this miracle, increase our faith to believe nothing is impossible with God. Amen.

Musical Bonus
Today we have a special treat. For King and Country gives *Joy to the World* a contemporary twist.
https://youtu.be/TPA0jTQI2HM

December 23

The Great Divider

> "Behold, this child is appointed for the fall and rising of many in Israel, and for a sign that is opposed"
>
> — Luke 2:34

CALL THIS THE BAD NEWS about the good news.

Not everyone loves Jesus.

Not everyone is glad he came.

The scribes ignored him.

Herod tried to kill him.

Their descendants will nail him to a cross.

He is the Great Divider of Men. He will cause many to fall. He will cause many to rise. Many will speak against him, and the hidden thoughts of the heart will be revealed.

What a thing to say about a tiny baby. "Mary, they are going to touch this child, and you won't be able to do anything about it. They are going to hate him, they are going to lie about him, they'll spread rumors about you and Joseph, they will smear his name with malicious lies. You will stand by helplessly and watch it happen."

It all came true.

Eventually they questioned not only his parentage but also his mental ability. They snickered and said, "He thinks he's the Son of God. But he's just filled with demons." When hatred took complete control, they arrested Jesus and put him on trial as a seditious blasphemer. They beat him within an inch of his life, leaving his skin in tattered ribbons. After the trial, he was condemned to die. In the end, Mary stood by the cross and watched her son die an agonizing, brutal, bloody, inhuman death. Amid the stench and gore of crucifixion, Mary stood by her son, unable to staunch the flow of blood, unable to wipe his brow, unable to hold his hand.

It all happened exactly as Simeon had predicted. When Mary watched her son die, a sword pierced her soul. *Above the cradle stands the cross.* This baby was born to die. Dag Hammarskjold, late Secretary-General of the United Nations, put it this way:

> How proper it is that Christmas should follow Advent. For to him who looks toward the future, the Manger is situated on Golgotha, and the Cross has already been raised in Bethlehem.

He was born to end up that way.

The way you respond to Jesus reveals your heart. But that's not all. The way you respond to Jesus tells us where you will spend eternity.

Gracious Lord, give me grace to take my stand with Jesus today and never be ashamed of him. I care not what others say. I will follow Jesus! Amen.

Musical Bonus
Phil Wickham sings the Christmas classic
What Child is This.
https://youtu.be/aITXBJ4vMrg

December 24

No Room

> "She brought forth her firstborn son, and wrapped him in swaddling clothes, and laid him in a manger; because there was no room for them in the inn"
>
> — Luke 2:7

No room in the inn.

How could that be?

For that matter, how could God let this happen? It seems like a terrible oversight to allow your only Son to be welcomed to earth with a "No Vacancy" sign.

But God knew what he was doing.

He was born like this so the humble might feel free to come to him. The very manner of his birth—turned away from the inn, born in a stable—means God welcomes the rejected, the abused, the mistreated, the forgotten, and the overlooked. "We might tremble to approach a throne, but we cannot fear to approach a manger" (Charles Spurgeon).

If Jesus had been born in Paris or Beverly Hills, only the rich and famous would feel at home with him. But since he was born in a stable, all the outsiders of the world instinctively feel a kinship with him.

Having no room in the inn is more than an incidental detail. *Indeed, it is central to who Jesus is.* Now that we know why he came, surely we will say, "He had to be born like this. It couldn't have happened any other way."

Is there a hint here of his upcoming death? I believe there is. Turned away from the inn and resting in a feeding trough, he was already bearing the only cross a baby can bear—extreme poverty and the contempt and indifference of mankind. In the words of Francis of Assisi, "For our sakes he was born a stranger in an open stable; he lived without a place of his own wherein to lay his head, subsisting by the charity of good people; and he died naked on a cross in the close embrace of holy poverty."

This baby lying forgotten in an exposed stable, resting in a feeding trough, is God's appointed "sign" to us all. This is a true incarnation. *God has come to the world in a most unlikely way.* This is what Philippians 2:7 means when it says that he **"made himself nothing, taking the very nature of a servant, being made in human likeness."** Nothing about the baby Jesus appeared supernatural. There were no halos, no angels visible, and no choirs singing. If we had been there, we might have concluded that this was just a baby born to a young couple down on their luck. Nothing about the outward circumstances pointed to God. Yet all of it—every part of it, every single, solitary, seemingly random detail—was planned by the Father before the foundation of the world.

To the unseeing eye, nothing looks less like God; to those who understand, God's fingerprints are everywhere.

There was no room for Jesus that night in Bethlehem. Will you make room for him in your heart this year?

My Lord, come and dwell in my heart today.
There will always be room for you! Amen.

Musical Bonus
The a cappella group Pentatonix has reimagined many Christmas carols. This arrangement of *Silent Night* might be one of their best.
https://youtu.be/sme8N2pzRx8

December 25

Great Joy

"But the angel said to them, 'Do not be afraid! For behold, I bring you good news of great joy that will be for all the people.'"

— Luke 2:10

GREAT JOY.

Sounds good, doesn't it?

We could use an extra helping of great joy right now. As 2024 lurches to a close, no one knows what the last few days will bring. Perhaps they will be peaceful and non-newsworthy, which would be a great surprise after the events of this year.

Political crisis.

Attempted assassination.

Recession fears.

Threats of world war.

Job loss.

Sickness.

Hurricanes.

Wildfires.

Floods.

The list goes on and on. The last twelve months have felt like crawling across a minefield blindfolded. Yet here we are, on Christmas Day, celebrating the birth of our Lord.

That means we made it. Somehow, we survived a difficult year. Take a deep breath. Relax. Exhale. Smile. Look around. You deserve a medal for hanging in there long enough to make it to Christmas Day.

On one of his speaking tours, Richard Neuhaus was picked up at the airport by a man who kept talking about how bad things were in America and how difficult these times are. Finally, Rev. Neuhaus had

had enough of the doom and gloom talk. "These may be bad times, but they are the only times we are given. And despair is a mortal sin."

Despair is not an option. Let's make that a rule for ourselves: No despair on Christmas Day! How can we be sad when Christ was born in Bethlehem?

All God has to say to us can be wrapped up in one word: "Jesus." And not just any Jesus, but only the Lord Jesus Christ revealed in the New Testament. *He alone is the Lord from heaven. He alone can save us.*

All God has for you and me is wrapped up in his Son. No matter what difficulties we face or the decisions we must make, God leads us back to that one-word answer: "Jesus."

In an interview with David Frost, Billy Graham said he hoped the last word he uttered before dying was simply this: "Jesus." We can't do any better than that.

Two thousand years ago, God sent a gift wrapped in swaddling clothes and lying in a manger. *Jesus is God's Christmas gift to you.*

Merry Christmas!
The happy day is here at last.
Joy to the world, the Lord is come!

Lord of all, we come before you, celebrating this happy day when Eternity entered time and the Infinite became finite. Give us ears to hear the glad tidings and voices to sing with exuberant praise that, at long last, our Redeemer has come! Amen.

Musical Bonus
We end our Advent journey with a newer Christmas song. Let's celebrate together as Michael W. Smith sings *Christmas is Here.*
https://youtu.be/ZjOHCDSECkk

Merry Christmas to one and all!

We hope you have enjoyed this journey through the Advent season!

Would you consider donating so we can continue to offer the electronic version of this book and thousands of other resources free to people around the world through our website?

Thank you, and God bless you!

Donate to Keep Believing Ministries
https://www.keepbelieving.com/donate/

www.ingramcontent.com/pod-product-compliance
Lightning Source LLC
Chambersburg PA
CBHW032059040426
42449CB00007B/1133

* 9 7 8 1 9 4 3 1 3 3 8 6 4 *